Instructions for an Animal Body

Instructions for an Animal Body

poems by Kelly Gray

MOON
TIDE PRESS

~ 2021 ~

Instructions for an Animal Body
© Copyright 2021 Kelly Gray

Editor-in-chief
Eric Morago

Editor Emeritus
Michael Miller

Marketing Director
Dania Alkhouli

Marketing Assistant
Ellen Webre

Proofreader
Jim Hoggatt

Front cover art
Douglas Pierre Baulos

Book design
Michael Wada

Moon Tide logo design
Abraham Gomez

Instructions for an Animal Body
is published by Moon Tide Press

Moon Tide Press
6709 Washington Ave. #9297
Whittier, CA 90608
www.moontidepress.com

FIRST EDITION

Printed in the United States of America

ISBN # 978-1-7350378-6-8

Contents

Foreword

The first time Kelly Gray took one of my writing workshops and read her work out loud, a spell was cast on the room. It rushed in like the wet chill of night. It was early in the dark of the new year and she was one of a dozen writers crammed into my living room, sipping hot tea and sharing words on paper. Every time we turned to workshop Kelly's writing, the group met her with deep sighs of admiration. Her stories and poems had their way with us all, gripping us, carrying us along for the ride.

Before that workshop, one of my first vivid memories of Kelly is meeting her along a path in the oak woodlands of Northern California. The dusty path led to a swimming hole near the camp we were both attending; we said hello and watched a mother deer and her young fawns just off the side of the trail. It was late summer, and we were deep in a thick and relentless heatwave. It was the time of year in California when one grows wary of the dragging on and on of the hot dry days and longs for the cool release of fall: coastal fog and long nights wrapping arms around us, pulling us deeper toward winter.

Kelly's writing feels like this. Kelly's writing *is* this: that longing being met, like crossing over the threshold into the wild comfort of ourselves.

When I think of my own longing, and the longing of others held back by expectations the world grips us with, I imagine the ways I want to cut loose, set myself free. And I know I can find that unleashing in and between and under the lines of Kelly's words. After reading some of her poems, I see myself howling out grief or tearing my clothes off and running barefoot across jagged rocks and the spines of dead wild things. I feel cold water wash over me as I dive into the dark blue of the sea. I feel the dryness of desert, the thickness of mud. They do these things to me, these poems. They are visceral, charged. They invite us into the depths of our raw, beautifully messy animal bodies.

She gets into the guts of what it's like to be a human animal, sometimes literally: fish, whale, snake, raptor; the acidic churning stomach of a bear. She reaches into the heaviness of vulnerability, holds you against shame and isolation, claws her way into the depths of lust, reveals the sharpness of loss. We all have this inside of us, and Kelly's writing brings us straight to it. Ushers what is aching into freeness.

Do not expect to read these words and fold them onto a shelf and walk away. You will step into them, become a part of each story's landscape, and they will become a part of you.

So, dear reader, find a nice space to settle in. Remove your shoes and let your bare feet sink into the earth (or into a stream or pond). Find a sturdy tree to lean back against. Let your hair down. Feel the wind against your skin. Clear your calendar. You won't want to leave these pages.

~ Dani Burlison
author of *Some Places Worth Leaving* and *All of Me: Stories of Love, Anger and the Female Body*

This is for the little girl who was told that being a healer is the work of prostitutes. Although this can be true, it's not true in the way that they meant it. Your hands vibrate medicine into the dark places of another's body.

This is for the girl who was told that her writing must be linear. Loop out, little one, and bring it full circle.

This is for all the people who have made me brave. For my father who drove me across the Mojave Desert floor listening to detective novels on cassette tapes, teaching me my first lessons in observation. For Zane, who pushed me to the front of the room. For the good people of Montana, who left me face-down in the snow to dig my way out. For my people who sit with me in the stillness after the scream. For my love and our shared home of fog. For my daughter, because we must be brave.

Introduction: Keeping Apparitions

There is a ghost for each crack of the child's heart. Her ghosts are neither good nor bad. They bless, they poison, they offer deliverance through wood and poetry, through empty buckets and walking sticks. The ghosts take the form of wild beasts, of her parents, of a long hallway, a warmth pressing between her legs. They are all things at once while reflecting her nothingness. They are born from her dreams where the she-monsters cry, where the mermaids drown, where the warm rush of his arms in the river made her see God.

We live in an unincorporated town with a busted-up post office housed in a trailer. There is a sign painted on a mossy rock that says, "This Way to Town" with a hand pointing nowhere. There is a mountain lion that wanders the dark trail behind my house. The cat-man with hundreds of empty tin cans spilling over his deck. The vulture sits above my house, black wings spread, drying herself off against the wet night. In her vomit we find finely cracked vertebrae and delicate femurs. Down the hill are old men with crumbling cabins and dry crab nets. The river shoots creeks in every direction, usnea drips green from trees, everything is pulled in and spit out by the forest. The ocean is 9 miles and seven fence posts away.

My home is quiet. The one-way street that curves over a bridge and through bramble is rarely walked. It is hard to be distracted from matters of the heart in this forest.

The abandoned child keeps ghosts in the steam of her bath water and in the space between one song and the next. She sleeps with aberrations pulling at her wrists, she wakes with ghost-kissed eyelids. They circle her patiently, blowing the hair out of her eyes, whispering moments of meaning into her lungs. She pauses in the pantry looking through empty jars of dried leaves. You used to belong, you used to belong.

At night I have a reoccurring dream that I have snuck into my family's home, past the taxidermied red-tailed hawk and the boar's head, through the glass library, and on to the couch facing the garden. I have come to sleep. In my dream I am ragged from a life of insomnia. The dream always ends without sleep. My family walks in and catches me, shames me for needing refuge, and then tells me to leave.

In the morning, I sit quietly waiting for my daughter to wake. I take these moments to make coffee and prepare the coat of mothering, a coat that always needs new stitching. In hopes of feeling less left, to ease the lines around my worried eyes, to feel the small of my hands in the large of his hands, I bring a man home. I show him the house cut in two by a fallen redwood tree.

I show him the heads and torsos at the sculptor's home. We find a torn deer leg on the trail left by the mountain lion. He pisses off my porch. We skin a snake in the creek bed; leave its body for the ravens. Shoulder, collarbone, shoulder. I bring him into my bed.

My dreams intensify around him. When he leaves in the morning, all the ghosts follow after him, so taken are they with the warm flesh of his neck. The deep wrinkles scented with dirt.

The jilted child is prophet. She sees through touch, she smells through images. At the side of your mouth, she can see your thoughts before they have been formed. This is her gift, to see the future. All things must die. All things are alone… but she has this memory, this memory of being born and belonging…

The comfort of his touch reminds me of being loved. Just a faint brush against my fear, but enough to hurtle me towards the inevitable. *Love is left and leaving,* they sang, *one in the same.* Not fully understanding the architecture of my lungs, he asks me to get behind my breath. I want my ghosts back. *Nail his hands to the walls,* they coo, *don't wash the sheets for his smell.* My ghosts threaten to leave me for him, so I chain my ghosts to the trees and asked him to go, even though I want him to stay.

The first three days after he leaves, I read about snakes and the art of transmuting poison. He produced a small crack and provided an articulation to my grief that I had not yet understood. *He became the faintest ghost of all, walking the woods, dragging bones and birds about him.*

On the fourth day, my ribs begin to break but my eyes are clear. I stand alone in the forest, finally able to see the outline of my family. I see my mother bend down above my bed with my journal in her hand. I see my grandmother's radio, the outline of her form as she paints hummingbirds on canvass. There is no space for silence within me, only a loud rushing. I miss my brother, perhaps most of all. I see him across the fire, holding up a fish from the sea, a gift to me that he used to bring me.

If you can see spirits then you can see the ghosts of girls walking in the woods, over the railroad tracks, pissing in plain sight. They are pulling apart your curtains, your construction sites, the wings of geese at the river's edge. Their song is painful; their voices pitched high and unfavorably against the night's dim light. But if you can see spirits, you will want them. You will want them more than your lovers, your family, yourself. You will chain them to trees, and make everyone leave, if only for a moment alone with them.

The Fox as Form

In my dream I am a grey fox with a rabbit in my mouth. I sense my human form in how much I must stretch my jaw to hold this limp warm body, all the fear twitching between my teeth and tongue, hair in the back of my throat. I walk past the cypress line to where the tall grasses grow. I can see a sliver of my human skin beneath a paw pad. There in the pressed grass is a family of deer; I hear two heartbeats. The mama deer twitches her ears against a scent and having failed many fawns in seasons past, she keeps her eyes wide with legs bent beneath her. I look at her, but we are not friends. We only inhabit the same space. I recognize the look in her eyes as sounds larger than loss swirl around us. In my dream the trees are talking to me, telling me to drop further to the ground, to take off my human clothes and stitch this fox skin around me.

My human body is old and smells like people I don't know. I place the rabbit aside and start to sew. First the fox ears, so I can hear where I am going. Then the legs, tightly, with beautiful stitching, so they don't become loose as I run. All the prey I chase will admire them. Next the tail, which is hard to get on correctly because of the bushy shape but I do, and I even hide the seam. I pick up the rabbit. Starting off again, through the mud, tightening my narrow jaw around my catch as the trees begin to smile.

Spread Horaltic // My Marking of the Hours //

My bird mentor says we are getting the turkey vultures out, but I couldn't. I was so tired, and they are so big, and I was bleeding so much. I just couldn't. But I knew they were coming. A friend sends me a poem, written about her life as a vulture, eating out the eyes of those who don't believe survivors of sexual assault. A friend who is mostly made of stars and poetry, loses a shadow made of cat bone. Now they only see empty space, and I cry as they tell me about their loss, and how we don't have space to grieve the animals we love more than ourselves. Another friend—she loses her baby—and I feel clenched up, thinking of all the loss, all the children, and the empty places that mothers mourn, even before we lose them. She speaks of tea with sister-sorrow and stepping into the dressing gowns of Mother Death, and I want to set the table for her, and pour her mugwort tea, but I know that I can't. I fall asleep weepy and with kind words being whispered in my ear, but you know how it is some days, it's just so hard if only because we love so much.

But this morning when I wake up, I walk outside, and the vultures fly up from the bramble, surrounding me in the trees. Six of them. I drink dark milky coffee and watch. Quiet beasts among the morning bird song. White beaks, for flesh. Wings that stretch for sun. Waiting for the thermals. Waiting for the smell of split skin. I remember her words, "It's the organ meat that gets me going, the heart of cow that makes me weak-kneed," and I know my friends are vultures, pulling apart all the loss, drinking tea, calm and quiet in the trees around me.

The Fish as Healer

I can only pray underwater,
and only after god drags my bright white nickeled knees
across the dark virescent floor of the estuary,
submerging me with watery benedictions,

asking, *is this enough?*
asking, *can you float?*

Me, gleaming against the algae,
hair escaping into murmurs the shape of current.
By the pressure of water my arms glide back seraphic,
my fingers catching in the sea grass.

Here, I pray for the sting of salt in my eyes.
Chin titled towards light breaking through water.
You know, all you can hear underwater is breath
and the sound of the heron's step.
The way the webbing pulls up against the mud, the intention of
sinking.
I want the washing, the ones babies get in utero,
gathering up all of our devotions and digressions against ourselves
before we are born into this world.
We arrive imperfect and howling.
We arrive wet.

Wound One:
Fingernails digging crescent moons into flesh,
unable to release a small arm.
Bring a salmon to that arm, one that has swam from sea to creek,
one who has laid eggs and tail flapped fertility into the rocks.
Skin that salmon once, then twice, to feed the child,
use those same nails to scrape the fish skin
so that ancient sea trails are embedded in my arms.

Wound Two:
The tied mouth.
Remove the threads carefully,
Slowly around the corner seams, find grace seeping
into the water as the prayer becomes articulated,
A small bubble rising.
I speak with fish.

I am not drowning. I float past the cormorant's legs.
The fish say, *The next wound is language. We are not fish.*
We are silver and flesh and bones and curves of slick.

Wound Three, As Taught by The Salmon:
Now that you are free words will weigh like rocks.
Rocks are only evidence of water.
We open our stomachs and rocks tumble out.
This is where we will lay our eggs.
Shiny bright jellied eggs.
Eggs like words.

Forgetting who is me and who is fish and who is listening,
we spawn words against our wounds
continuing to drag our bodies against the rush of warm water
at the juncture of our confluence.
We kneel without knees
with new bodies given to us by our own work
as the birds and bears descend
to feed on our healing
so that the trees may know the river floor.

Bear Need

There was once a bear who needed me so within the acidic warmth of her digestion that she chased me up & over the mountain top, across ridges made of shattered volcanos, snow to my knees, a rope for the crevasse I could not see. I would place my hands inside her tracks and look at the trees where I thought I could see her face, but it was just the way a tree will look at you with all the eyes of twisted bark.

I collected moss to place between my legs, soaking up my blood scent with the green of wildwood, then burned it in the lick of the fire, letting my fertility smoke up across the snow-blown mountain night. How she wanted to see me pregnant, how I avoided this calling.

My bear was right outside the fire's light, watching me eat flour and onions from my hands. She loved me so hard she chased me strong with those beastly shoulders smelling of musk and roots. That's what we think, that to devour is to love, till we learn the breath of beast as teeth sink.

For years that bear chased me till my feet cracked and a day came that I made my way down off that mountain, stumbling to the flatlands, where the men had guns, and I called back up to her: *next time.*

The Hart

He steps out of the grass like a god. Thick necked to hold up east-to-west spanning antlers which in turn hold up the entire sky, three clouds and a Northern Harrier. I am caught off guard by his emergence, how he came from nothing into everything. His softest places glow with the low cut of winter light; slow blinking eyes, the velvet of his antlers, his wet nose. He invites me to follow him down the trail, which I do. We walk slowly, stepping carefully through the grass, deeply aware of our shared breath. We are prey, not predator. The sun is beginning that low drop into the sea, breaking apart into pink and gold, catching in my eyes. Between the cliffs and the horizon is whale breath, one after another, a family. For a moment I feel this deep sense of kinship. I want to lie down in the grass and fold this connection around me and tie it into my boots and wear it like the old faux fur coat of my late teens. Did you have a coat like that? One that you could wear like a home? I miss that heavy coat anchoring me while I wandered fields in the dark, wrapped up like I belonged to the land.

The Places Inside Me

I am beginning to creep with my monster. It will take me
to the jagged rocks and I'll lick the salt

off of them. I'll stick my hand in the falcon's face
because I am so fucking dead it makes me alive

three times more. Three times more I get to die.
I ask the trees, *what do I do?* and they say leave all this shit behind

come into the world of monsters. We have always been here.
We are the bloody snouts of coyotes

that live by the law of leaving. *Just leave me alone,* you said.
So, I did.

I-395

In the beginning, there was only you
and your knife. You start by carving out a landscape,

a place to hang your words. Chip by chip you design a desert floor
and then, the inverse dome of black sky.

A thin needle pluck for every star, which may take the most
time of all, to conceive of a thousand myths in needlepoint.

You build a truck to travel that gash of a highway I-395 Inyo County,
with a grooved bed and small cab, and impregnate a woman

with two children, placing one, asleep, in the back of the truck
with a pillow and dog.

Beside you, you place the other child awake,
making sure she can only see the edge of the desert in the headlights

because you don't bother
to make any plants or animals or distractions,

not even the bodies of coyotes who eventually come for her.
Anyway, for now she is midnight trucking,

reeling at a 90mph lullaby
because some bedtime stories need to be told beneath the level of the sea.

You hang a helicopter in the sky, right above the truck,
flexing your fatherhood, godhood

to move pitch and machines across continents and time.
You, the original Storyteller.

You bring back in time that same knife Army
issued circa 1965 combat medic knife and a Boy

in your arms that you had swept off the jungle floor
all hovering and messed up in the sky of then untranslatable myths.

It turns out you needed a black sky to tell this story all along.

There was no anesthesia, only the difference
between what you would do and couldn't do,

and your ability to know that this moment would be retold
to your daughter, even as he cried out against you

thinking this was your story as you amputated his arm,
and placed your moment and his moment

into the small of your child's back as she looks sideways at you as you
drive your truck across this world

that she had mistaken as yours,
while you tell her stories of how god creates men.

Cetology

Whales have flexible rib cages that bend without breaking, drawn by design for diving deep without collapsing under pressure. Your rib cage: impossibly rigid with lungs that bleed in deep waters. Not even that deep in the sea, you and me. If a whale were measuring, we'd be done in the shallows. But the heart of the whale, that car of a heart that beats once every ten seconds. Large enough for us to find refuge in while we drown. Can you hear it? The impossible whooshing of the greatest pause of blood on earth in our ears, you curled up in the right aorta, me in the left ventricle, feeling the surge, counting to ten until our ribs crack, a wall of membrane between us.

The Blue Blood of a Bolete

The truth of the mushroom is that it's an expression
of the underworld, the tender lick of umami

fruit, grown in the shadow land.
There is a certain marvel at the explosive nature
busting up through wet leaves and smelling like the liminal

space between then and now.
This is what happens when you send your death to the soil,
when you bury your lover.
Nooooo, shush, not their body—

but the idea of them.
Conceding that that they were only ever an idea,

you walk into the forest of Autumn, with your switch blade
or hatchet, or maybe just your ungloved hands and a spoon.
You were never prepared for this part of the story.

So, you start digging, past the lovers from before,
through a catacomb of squirrel bones,
the places where your fingers bleed.
You mix him with nutrients and lore of the soil,

with worm shit and pine needles,
all the layers of your torn dresses

and his one sock
that you keep moving around the house,
unable to throw it out. You keep digging

till you find that bright white highway of
mycelium and goodbye,
and you leave him there with all his exposed hypha
while he dies. Again, this is just

the idea of him. But he is there
dying in the underworld of the forest,

and you come back a week later to find him,
bursting forth in new form,
edible but toxic, bleeding blue,

not at all the thick stiped mushroom you were looking for.

Trace Tracking

This way, off the trail. Spine, pelvis, skull. She picked up the sacrum and sighed at its familiarity. We walk with fawn jaws in our pockets.

She wants to know how he saw the kestrel pellet tucked into the grass and glistening with beetle wings. With repetition you see patterns. Then, it's a softening and a scanning. You can feel it in your palms and the weight of your heel. Pause. Your peripheral vision is your third eye, it pulsates but does not blink. Lower. She drops into her animal body.

Augury

The raven Tiresias is telling secrets at the bar, six drinks in and two snake strikes behind them, they lost their gender in the bathroom, their eyesight in the alleyway.

But I am walking creaky-legged trying to get home when they fly up next to me, and they lean in—bend in—can't quite tell if this is man or bird but they have this way of opening their mouth so wide, asking me to count the feathers that travel down their open beak to the back of where their bra is showing.

I have to look in to see for myself, tongue black wet, back of throat black, glassy green eyes made of milk. This bird sees birds, throws sparrow wings to the sky and cries out *this is truth, this is death, I am blind!*

I'm just trying to get laid but you're talking to me like you know me, bird.

The raven puts its cigarette out in the entrails of a smashed starling found behind the wheel of a Cadillac.

Their eyes roll back into their head and the smell of burned wings makes me lick-lip hungry, they start to tell me a story that I already know but forgot ten years back at another bar. I interrupt them, so lush with rice whiskey and steeped cherries that golden poppies spill from my lips, so full of blossoms they can smell my unfolding within the containment of a body without wings.

I just want to know,
my own pleasure, *where did it go?*
The bird pulls back to look at my face, petals falling from my eyes.

Yes, Tiresias, I remember (now) how we met. You flew into the shutters, almost dead on the floor among the suitcases and cassette tapes. I took your body in my hands, tied my words to your feet,
marked your beak with my blood.

I released you through the window in hopes you would fly my letters home across oceans and rooftops, scattering blood from my wrists so that no one family would feel the weight of my burden.

Now, you've come back, to tell me what you know of me. To right my two-wronged way, to caw up my skirt and untie me from this gold rotted city where I've been held flat against the hills, almost dead on the floor.

Now, it's your turn. Unbind my eyes from the ground, release me from the relentless growl of a thousand sleeping babies, all their mothers pushing against doors to keep the sound of the sky from descending lest they begin to wake, starved.

We can fly these streets together, opening all the doors, rattling bassinets, grabbing pigeon after pigeon to toss their bodies to the streetlights like a map of bird light leading us past slayed snakes and the intersection of Geary and 20th where I held him when he died.

Tempt me out of this body
holy untold
bound for joy
promise me it's here in the prophecy.

Promise me, Tiresias, you'll take me home tonight, to show me what I cannot see. They hop, bird-like, human-like, foot to foot, wrapping a black wing around me, nest bound.

The Cypress and the Harrier

You find me as a cypress tree riven by lightening,
dropped accessible in the night tender
growth and dark bark opening
as an offering up to the stars—

a history of draughts and the structure of streams against my roots,
the circles of my heartwood. This is the place where you climb
inside of me, moving up to find a hive buzzing
behind my knees, lace lichen in the corner of my closed eyes,
corvid nests woven from my hair.

Half my trunk is enough to build
you a home, wood that you are going to take
as if I am a grove. Your rusted bow saw behind your back
measuring my circumference as you groan,
creep among my needles digging
your heels into my twisted grooves marked
by the sapsucker, smelling of lemon.

Dawn breaks, pulling birds from my mouth,
you persist on.

Half my trunk bent
over in our bed of winds, humbled by the relentless ocean
pushing whales bones up the continental shelf
that we can't see, but you told me you *could*

see me
as you pressed me into dirt, my bark
between your fingers between my legs between my cliffside sheets
that we keep having to bleach
white in the sun to remove
stains from my sap running down
your face as you lap up

my life,
forcing me to expose every ring after ring,
circling in, back to the hills that the harrier sweeps over.

We pause.
The harrier.

Low in flight past our own harried flight, the attention
paid by this bird to the coastal prairie,
to the twists of grass, flush of vole,
showing her wings this way and that way

to the sun. She drops into the rifts cut open by quakes and coursing
water, she glides low, and head bound down
lo,
lo,
lo.
She can't look away.

And I look to you for the first time, thinking
as trees do,
that I have never been loved.

Carcass

My friend told me, "There is a fawn carcass behind your cabin." I knew the mother, sat and walked with her while she was pregnant, so I wanted to pay my respects. But before I got there, I had a dream about a bobcat with a man leaning low, brushing his hand across the cat's head as they inspected the fawn. I asked them not to move the bones, but you know how cats are. Maybe some men, too. This morning, it took me awhile to find it. It had been pulled deeper into the forest. But here it is, small and still giving of marrow. I knelt to pay respect to the fawn, the bobcat, and the man.

Mascot Masquerade Ball

They took my body into the bowels of the football team,
raised me like a flag from the outhouse
to a party where my knees buckled,
tongue brazen as the bold lettering of jacket number 37,

they pinned me 14 hands and wall,
told my breasts they were too soft,
coached on like pep
like rally,
like soda stitched cafeteria sick—
where will you eat lunch now?

Expelled for throwing books
in the deep recess of Psych 101,
pages as open as my legs held by
definitions not yet brought on by cultural commentary of new day.

All the girls said we will never love you now,
you suck dick like trick; you're kind of like a boy.
Hungry.
Cheering like dolls with
cheap lips and volley
net as my disguise,

I should have torched your hallways
at the first slap of slut,
dragged my nails across the locker room bench
wet with stench sweat told holy by a team
as you shot
spitwad cum into the back of our necks,
while we penned essays on Joseph Conrad, "The horror, the horror!"

All the baby queer bois, the angriest of us all,
up the hill working hard to look like
tractor cut grass
invisible bend overs stuck in the slur of a neck turned red—
I remember his knuckled notes from across the aisle.

I should have slit your throat
twenty-five years later when across from me in a new class,
me as the teacher while
you still look like gold,
soft like agriculture slipping across a hill.

Instead, I taught you to hold your wife's face
as she labored your son that I could feel in the swell of her belly,
I pulled your hands to her hips and said into the space between the two of you,
no not like this, hold her here, so she does not fly away.
I touched your hands like you didn't rape that boy blind.

Do you remember me? I asked you.
Naaaaaah, you said, as you blinked back the recognition of my childhood.

Cantus Mycena
Common Name: Siren Fungi, Singing Mycena

These little mushrooms are known for their whale-like songs that they emit during rain showers. Mycologists have recorded songs lasting more than three minutes in length, barely audible to the human ear. The songs have a precise beginning, middle, and end, and often grow louder in the days leading up to the full moon. First recorded in the early 1900s during the Acoustic Era* of recording, the songs were previously thought to have been forest spirits inhabiting decaying trees. Many still know this to be true, and we encourage you question your reaction to the validity of scientists, this writing, and fungi as distinct species in general. The songs will change in tone and duration depending on who is listening, and although they usually have a lush, dark, and watery quality (some say reminiscent of the days that Nick Cave and PJ Harvey shared a bed and pen), they are known to develop a shrill or agitated quality around groups of men in uniforms wielding clipboards or axes. Large clusters are thought beneficial to certain lichens and mosses that only reproduce when vibrational frequencies warm their spores during rainstorms which acts to dislodge them, making the perfect combination for dispersal in the last remaining coastal redwoods of the Pacific North West.

Although most musicians struggled with low fidelity and volume, thus resorting to louder instruments such as trombones, scientists in the field were surprised to find that the large conical horns, often mimicking the shape of the fungi, seemed to register the low fungal frequencies and that they had very few sonic limitations.

Termite Moon

When the woman turns the bedside light off, it is still bright. The Moon has crept through the sky and made way through the forest, round-faced and looking into the woman's room. The Moon places yellow-lighted hands on the small home and shakes it. The rats in the walls squeal, moon-splinters seep through wood and glass, termites and spiders turn their little faces skyward.

'Get up', the Moon says.

'I cannot,' the woman replies, 'I must close my eyes and go where bodies go when they sleep.'

'No,' the Moon says. 'You can lay awake, and your shallow imagination will arrive regardless. You can worry about your heart, the way it's only half a heart, and I will crest from East to West. It is best that you stay awake for this.'

'No,' the woman moans, gripping her pillow. She must rest. The Moon touches her blankets, her cheeks, blows on her feet, whispers up her legs.

'You are alone,' the Moon notices, touching the place on the bed the woman avoids.

'I thought we were together,' the woman says to the Moon, hurt.

'I am only a reflection of a day that's already been had,' the Moon responds.

The woman opens the window and asks the Moon in for the night. But when the Moon comes in, the woman slips out. She wanders down to the flooded river, and looking up, sees no stars. Looking down, they have fallen into the water. She spends the rest of the night pulling celestial bodies from the mouths of fish, untangling them from strands of algae. She takes handfuls and scatters them to the skies above, offering them back to the myths that had lost them. The Moon sleeps in her bed, content with pillows and blankets made of wool.

Her Name Was Amy

I had a babysitter who threw kittens into the pool from the balcony. Short shorts and hair sideways boombox convertible cigarette. The way she would sing and wink, like I wasn't there. Men with ink and greased ease, a leer for her bend, denim fringed inside thigh, smooth.

I think I loved her more than the kittens. Even when they went under and came up to float, mewing wet like they had just been reborn. *You better run down and get them.* My bare feet slapping on 1950s apartment building cement, gathering them up into her borrowed yellow crop top, soaking with claws and pinprick. Pit hungry because there were no snacks.

Me looking up at her, saying with my eyes, *I saved them, I saved them.*

The Cartography of Syzygy

For a millennium, men have laid their hands
  dusted with hematite
    in the cave of my thighs,
      reaching up to paint the conquest of their kill:
a three-legged ungulate,
a flint blade,
forewarnings of the deerstalker, my bed made of bones.
I am a vast system, inexorable,
  and you with no rope.
    They've drawn maps across my ribs,
      marked the fork in my rivers,
seen my sigh as a weather system.
Two hurricanes in particular,
the way they wrapped cheap serpent rings around our fingers
as we met between your first and my last ritual.
  You held me by the throat 'til
    my tongue broke into parchment paper
      and pulling it out
the symbols swooped and dived with my spit.
You just sat there reading me
the warning signs:
  my ankles marked by the water lines of lunar tides
    a tsunami in the palm of your hand
      our fluvial floods spanning the back of my thighs.
All the ancient markings and dead birds you promised I would
drag out behind me
and throw at your feet.
But then you only birthed daughters
  who you could never teach my slander to,
    who you could never tell me about,
      as if I didn't know
their forms in my dreams.

Pulling Bastard

Come here, monster child. I lead weary. I take your hand and look at your knees. Your ankles with flea bites, your eyes cocked.

Come here, monster child, I see you in me, give me your palm. We lick piss into prayer. We lick like our hearts are made of milk. We lick like three is infinity, but we know that it was only ever: not like that, not like this, put that down.

Come here, monster child, with your crown of busted. Let me straighten your collar and see the underside of your chin. The place where your laughter is catapult rock. Unhinged you say, me with my sewing kit. Needles for eyes.

Two breaths like blow. Dust settles again on the shoulders. Don't be so mechanical with your brain like a machine. Our rusted smarts. I'll dive backwards into the pool, dreaming of gators. I offer a leg.

The Hush of a Switchblade

Let me write quite for you, two line stanzas
as if we have time left in this world for measured sentiment.

I hesitate, even, to bring your knife to this poem,
though I carry it carefully as Last Language

sung cliffside, sharp words pointed away from you.
I cut an X into the flesh that separates me from your breastbone,

wanting to know the delicate meat of your ribs.
Do you see me fleeting as ghost, you as child scuffed,

us on bike and vine?
I carve, to whisper to your wound,

delivering to your heart small wooshes of anatomy laid bare by
maps drawn anew: you are universe whole, all stars and ligament.

Those lips, fields of dirt that I drag my knees across,
the space of your mouth an ocean of squid and whale.

Your knuckle-scarred hands weather,
myth and death in the slung mud of your downpour.

Me, with too many eyes and a sword for a tongue,
each of us kneeling for no one, you were only ever a child,

undoing prayers like behemoths feasting on gods,
our bellies full, the quiet of the poem devoured.

The Season of Motherhood

My daughter is gust across field
with liquid sky eyes,
so bright she runs the brush of blackbird song against my ears.

We intersect where the long grass is ice flat
and snaps underfoot.
My land is Winter.
Voles sleep unseen deep beneath the dirt,
curled to the cold.
She is holding up peeling bulbs of flowers that we cannot name
by their earth-soaked artery roots.

She is walking forward,
away from my stillness,
my lungs punctuated with sad poems and a pile of unclaimed bones
as I am always, always
watching for moments of myself to guard her against.

She moves with her moon-white face tilted towards the ridge,
dragging me with her eyes towards Spring.

When the Shooter Comes: Instructions for My Daughter

I want you to crouch like a badger.
Drop deep into your animal body
to become broad and flat.

Dig your sett in the dirt and crawl into the dark.
Wrap yourself with worms and mycelium,
he may not see you in the tangled roots.
You will hear his footsteps vibrate above,
be quiet, be quiet, be quiet.

Listen, we don't have time for your human needs.
Do not call me,
I know that you love me.
Hold the thickest book to your heart,
and remember when I read to you.

Forget all metaphor and go deep into the closet.
Sit still as the broom
and steady your breath.
Think of the opossum,
your favorite animal,
emitting the smell of decay to trick the predators
among us.

I'll think of your small hands,
wrapped in wool,
as we drive the cold roads to school.

Keep You Here

I want to put you in a glass jar
with your pink cheeks and spider leg lashes.
They might call this child abuse,
but I don't care anymore.

You would be perfectly beautiful,
placed by my houseplants and books,
your little hands pressed against glass,
voice, muffled but sweet,
like soft chalk buttermint candy.

I would move you around the house,
by the window while I do dishes,
on the hutch while I read.
Not too close to the fireplace,
and I would wipe the steam away post bath.

It wouldn't be any jar.
I'm talking French green glass,
the lightest hue,
with a metal hinge and heaviness.
Unbreakable glass made for canning,
having lived a life in a field flung farmhouse,
now yours.

But really,
my fear is what if I don't come home,
my last breath against asphalt or worse, in the tubes of an aspirator,
and you are in this jar,
alone,
looking up at the world beveled,
and I haven't shown you all the books,
haven't read to you Leonora Carrington,
forgot to show you how to water the plants.

Which could lead you to choose,
a life in a jar
away from the world without me.

So, I offer you a glass of water instead,
reminding you (me) to hydrate.

Saudade, A Counter Manual
to be read before it's over or begun

You are working with the presence of absence.

When your despair takes away your hunger:

Hold your memory of her sideways and lay her down at your feet. Kneel beside her, stroke her hair behind her ears, and move low so that your hearts align. Take the memory of her breath and knead it into warm morning bread, like a tenderly experienced embrace, so that you might eat once again.

When you have become lost:

In that space before you know the flesh of her lips, paint a painting of your love for her with mountains and rivers and valleys, so that when she has left you, you might come back and walk in the landscape of her being and feel known.

When you must find shelter:

Become an architect in the face of her sidewalk shadow. Stencil in the curves of her knees beneath the breakfast table on tracing paper, draw your home in the palms of her hands as she sleeps. Lay a foundation with the memory of her hair, wet against her cool neck as she floats besides you in the river. Build a bathroom like the one where you took pictures of her wearing a silk kimono with flowers in her hair. Take the tub from the beach house, where she lay after you first told her that you loved her, and the tiles from the cottage in Mexico where she walked with burned feet after visiting the priestess. Hang curtains from the hotel where she snorted coke and drew moths all night long while you read *The Effects of Living Backwards*. Build a home where your children that she will never have can run and play without being told to hush. Plant a garden and hang a plank swing with ropes from the oak tree so that she will have a place to weep as you stand in your kitchen looking out at her fading form. Build hallways long enough to capture her laugh so that you might remember what it sounded like, and so that you have a place to pause between each room that will never know the heat of her body.

When you have no place to sleep:

Take that moment before what she loves about you is yet your flaw and build a bed out of it. Nail the pieces of her belief in you together, sand the planks of her courage for seeing your rawness smooth, and lay the softness of the impossibility of her loyalty down as a place to lie as the world goes cold once she has walked away. This will be your only bed, your only refuge, so build it strongly in the moment before she sees you.

When you are too cold to move:

Remember how bright the sun was as it slanted sideways through the curved window and across her face. Mark your memory as the airplane tilted with turbulence and she gripped your hand. Resurrect from your throat the image of her throwing back her beloved pills with a small plastic bottle of vodka, her fingers never letting go of yours. Remember how you could feel the sun and take that warmth and weave it into a blanket to wrap around the memory of you both in the sky, as close to the sun as two people could be.

1900

There was a field of sunflowers in Arezzo
where we used to bring our journals and undress
our breasts to show them to the sun
spinning around with fractured light in our eyes
pushing our nipples against the thick stalks,
dancing, all of us, humans and flowers
sharing the dirt walked on by fascists and made into a film
five hours and twenty minutes long
shown in irony
during a week in art class
taught by our beloved teacher
who eventually threw his body off the walls of San Gimignano
where he took us to see what real torture was,
places we could never dance
knowing what we did of
the sight of
flower fields outside our locked chambers.

On Becoming A Whale

First you must take your ear-bones
and consider the sound of the seashell
rolled up with echoes of future song.

Cut out your elbow.

Detach your pelvis from your spine
and let them float in the space of your body.

This is your reentrance fee to the
original amniotic fluids.

There was once a whale that said
I will not go back to land,
I will not go back.

The Serpent Lies

The operation to speak with forked tongues is simple, a fine slicing between intention and impact starting along the center depression of the tongue to where it roots in the throat. You can use a simple gold-plated x-acto blade sold at fine stores for this very purpose. Or, you can remove your moral compass, pull out its glass plate and shatter it across the pavement with the heel of your boot. If you're even near pavement. If you even have a moral compass, the kind with a glass plate that will shatter sharp enough to cut a tongue.

Your tongue. A snake wearing boots.

And then you will be a two-telling-story holder in your slithered ways, hang a brass-plated rattle tail from your neck as warning: I smell stories in three-dimensions. But you'll have to know your audience and that some of them can transmute poison from serum into breath; the dear sweet opossum in a twist of fate, bifurcate themselves ~with their three birth canals and wombs~ who remain resistant to your venom.

They don't care how you build your stories against the forest floor of metaphor.

You also need to know your history and *that* they won't sell you, you'll have to reimagine who cut your tongue in the first place, having forgotten you did it to yourself you'll want to tell everyone that it was a god or a group of gods, that you were held down on your back with bright lights in your face and scripture against your scales but actually you're wrapped up in an old book of idioms looking back at grammatical errors that indicate the slinging of mud and your tongue which is two is infected at the root where it use to be used to hold down a people

who had to cut their own tongues and you're starting to choke on the etymology and there is a fork in your mouth feeding you story after story until your body is so full you are wrapped in your own uroboros not knowing the difference between stories of death and stories of birth.

But actually, you're wrapped up in an old book of idioms
looking back at grammatical errors
that indicate the slinging of mud
and your tongue which is two
is infected at the root
where it use to be used to hold down a people

who had to cut their own tongues
and you're starting to choke on the etymology
and there is a fork in your mouth feeding you story after story
until your body is so full you are wrapped in your own uroboros
not knowing the difference between stories of death and stories of birth.

25 Acts of Relentlessness

1. My fear of death, but really my way of tricking you into thinking I welcome death
2. The rot of capitalism in my Post Office Box, while we still have a Post Office, my stack of bills that I leave until the box is so full, they threaten to revoke it
3. My period, the way I ruin sheets once a month
4. Zombies, I am told it is a hallmark
5. The sound of the ocean while camping, unable to sleep, left wide-eyed by the wait for the next wave to break
6. When you close your eyes to listen to the sound of the plague and hear the rubbing of a thousand insect wings in the architecture of liberalism refusing to wear masks as you know the locusts have arrived in the form of women who refer to themselves as goddesses
7. The death of pets, specifically
8. My child needing to be fed
9. My hair needing to be dyed
10. The longest wait as coffee grinds, water boils
11. My anxiety pooling in a divot in my stomach carved out by people who are now dead, or that act dead, people that scream at me from graves beneath my feet which are really just empty spaces waiting to be filled with bodies who no longer want to be near me
12. Dreams about tsunamis that originate from swimming pools filled with gators and the crumbling seaside cliffs that we used to walk beneath, collecting garbage and bull kelp to build sculptures of sea witches
13. My mother's voice caught in my throat
14. Waking every night at 11pm, gasping for air, hearing plates broken above my head
15. My desire to eat pink donuts
16. My desire to eat pink
17. My desire to eat
18. My desire
19. My capacity to impose beauty where there is none

20. My capacity to stand up when all I want to do is get gut
    punched so hard that I can't do anything but lay on cool
    linoleum looking at the underside of a sink that holds the water
    of my face that I apply and reapply every day
21. My capacity for curiosity, wondering how many people are gut
    punchers
22. My need to suck the spit from his mouth through the hole in
    his cock
23. The sixth day, for on the sixth day I feel the grip in my chest,
    the whisper that says, "You will lose something today, by scythe
    or by text, by tree falling on your home"
24. My asking: Did I love enough? Will they forget my mother's
    voice in my throat? Will they think that I was kind?
25. The bill from my therapist that ensures I have six more days
    that I can look at my roof without the pull of my psoas
    collapsing me into a position that they said I did fetal even
    though I am pretty sure that even there, maybe especially
    there, I was swimming backwards eating pink tsunamis of
    broken plates wondering why all the magic happens in the
    days after death like my blood in the shape of a valentine
    caught in the sheets of my bed, relentless

The Celebrations of Ravens

I read the elephants are drunk
in the Yunnan Province,
sloshed and sleeping in the tea gardens.
So bold they were to crush through villages and glass,
in the moments we turned our faces
to lay down with illness.

I heard the flowers are planning a super bloom,
sending messages of blossom revolt,
passing out scat and seed pamphlets,
forget-me-knots working the corner fields,
red-hearted poppies blasting manifesto;
their headlines read:
Free from Their Gaze.

In the canals of Venice
the water runs green with fish,
dolphins swim against stolen gold of Byzantium,

and I walk this forest,
resisting the urge to call it my own.

Today the ravens came,
seventeen of them
like black arrows through the sky,
flip tripping on the clouds so full of spring storm,
and all of us below,
renaming what was never ours to name.

Yesterday,
the vultures dropped down,
winking and descending low,
asking me, *is today the day?*
I remember the first time he took to my arm,
our mutual inquiry so close,
his broad wings wrapped around me,
prayer-blasted sun,
me thinking, this is so intimate
to be caught in the vulture's shadow,
his black embrace.

Noticing, his eyes like mine,
but this whole time,
it's been me,
death in a pink dress.

He's been so kind,
letting me drive these
human roads
past the humility of his work,
thinking that these highways lead to forever.

Crack Me Electric

In morning dark, my eyes open to the sound of frothing
sky beasts dragging their tic-bitten bellies
across rooftops and canyons, blast cracking their cloven
hooves against forest canopy, all wet
snout and bellow.

This is how thunder learns to feast on the fat of my dubiety.

The throat growl of storm rattles dead wood, lending
dreams of fire, lightning spit begins to fly.

This is how trees learn to die, branches aflame.

Between the bright flashes, I press my ear to his letter,
You should have been more contained, in ink

on screen he wrote.

This is how he learns to pour gas across my bed, canister tipped empty.

With nothing but soaked sheets caught on form I rise, through
doors I have slammed before, I come to the storm, to greet
the beasts on knees.

I am not praying. I am licking earth.
Dragging my own belly against granite and root, crest bound
to the top of the rock, dropped by a glacier as cold as my mouth
open in the night-
hollow.

This is how I learn that my internal etymology has shaped my
adaptations
from insect to monster.

I break my right arm,
     crack.   I break my left arm,
     crack.   I unhinge my hips,
     snap my ankles back to walk on the tops of my feet,
     wobbled.

I scratch at my brow till my third eye is revealed,
    then another   and   another   and   another.
Cheek,   cheek,   chin.
I reach within my mouth to pull up a rib from my torso,
Hold it to the sky, the lightning touches down, lighting my rib ablaze,

So, you can see me now,
and look, here in the light you can tell,
I was never held that together.

This is how I teach myself to see my broken form in the dark.
And yet, there is skin. Soft flesh, bone sugar
for marrow seeping skin, I soak
the poisoned veils worn by the Mushroom Gods,
wet their throats with my decay
so that my story may be washed through the dirt of day after day
in the thick of the plague
to be translated to the Underworld,
reminding the darkness that I used to be light.

This is how I teach myself; I am whole.

I gather my ligaments and bind broke,
I call up my snarl and sing pretty,
I take the gas and light.

This is how I learn to start fires, me looking up at the beasts who
birthed me.

Random Updates from the Time of Timeless

-Part One-

To start, there is a bat and Osprey sharing the same sky above me as the sun breaks fire light sideways in Mendocino. Sea lions can be heard and I'm getting torn up by mosquitos because I didn't pack anything with sleeves. My cat is being driven to my daughter's best friend's house, because fire is suddenly everywhere. Yesterday, everything felt electric, cracking magic and omens like I could have swallowed the storm that was delivered just for me. But just now, I told my daughter "Just smell the fucking flowers." There is a buck and doe watching me behind a field of naked ladies, the most pink I have ever truly seen. I've been wanting out of my little home so badly and now that I can't get back I feel sick, I didn't do a proper goodbye. Not that a goodbye is in order, but one gets accustomed. And just now, I'm not even kidding you, a fox ran up to where I'm sitting and just looked at me, which is not a huge surprise because I stepped in its shit earlier this morning. In typical single mom fashion, I'll have to wait to get in the shower to cry, because some things just make me cry—protests, riots, fire skies, and having my dad map out evac routes for me. It's like all love and loneliness these days. It's only mid-August. Fuck.

-Part Two-

I'm basically surviving off of Ethiopian food and coffee, which is lovely and earthy and grounding and does not require my cooking. My daughter has taken to figure drawing, sketching naked body after naked body. There is a certain vulnerability and movement to her work that exists in stark contrast to what's happening in my own body. I feel like metal. I have to remind myself to unlock my jaw. I walked to two parks yesterday and was reminded of how the world just keeps on, seemingly unaware of the fires a bridge over, layers of evacuation memory blurring. A little boy ran up, catcher's mitt on. "Cool dog," he throws to us, nodding. I want to tell him everything, just because he's another human in front of me and I haven't seen people in a few months. "Thanks," I say, reminding myself I don't know him. The dog lurches forward, they have a brief moment before I start to drag us away. The only thing that makes me feel connected to my community is the smell of smoke in the air, which I can only smell the moment I step outside, before it normalizes in my senses. A friend texts me that they can't read the maps anymore. We wonder about cognitive functions under trauma. I like lots of cream in my coffee, how it hits black and swirls and for a moment you feel like you can see the future, like you are fortune teller, like someone in your past read tea leaves and bird wings. Still, you didn't see this coming. The coffee never said a thing.

Apt. #829

My bones broke fire in the apartment
building of my body, no fancy rafters
just flickering lights and dead flies in my windowpane eyes.
Furniture like couches. Mirrors with no frames. Microwave.
The tracks of drag across carpet.
The alarm circling in the hallways of my arms.
Face down on the linoleum of the bathroom,
that one cool spot
against the all the rage.

Last Story

Let me fear on the body of spider. Not the spirit of them, not the essence, just obscene roundness, haired. Unable to usher them out, I settle to invite them in, letting wilted bodies decompose~ window side, corner wood and ledge, multitudes gather.

I think *This is the end of times*, my child's small form pressed against mine in the corner of house, sheltered from viewing that which we know is falling. The dead deer behind the fence, our creek dry, our elder neighbor left to wander.

I offer a palm to translucent body with spinnerets and fangs, small-pawed and bent-legged. A storyteller, like me, weaving traps. I observe her walk from finger to wrist, more coordinated than my motherhood.

Two sets of legs, one right, one left, follow each other. The others move recklessly, or maybe hopefully, it is hard to tell from this perch of human body where I wait, aversion kissed fingertips, child brought to chest, watching quietly as I summon the spider. Personal eschatology playing out in the dusted minutia of lost reverence.

Home of Seamstress

I am lungs of house, a glass-spanned wall hung chandelier of larynx and trachea, each breath bringing minutia of volcano particles, soil-slanted light, call it dust at noon.

I am mouth of house, tilted bookshelves, titles decorated with bird song, poet's ink, screaming to open bound tombs assuring me of want, as dry as my mouth is.

I am bowels of house singing pretty with apparitions who have haunted these hallways all along, water heater creak louder than boot-kick can fix, begs of stomach, flesh pipes.

Linked between eyelids, teeth made of tendons, broad planks of wood, a tub to wash words in, clawed.

I am hollow of house, needlewoman, double crossed on floor, spilled eyes and fabric scraps each stitch pushing blood into seams of curtain drawn across crowds of mannequins and fruit eaters.

Only tea cloth pressed to inner thigh receives blood chimney and embroidery, my kettle rattles against closed door of home.

Fog Bank

I knew a boy whose name was Sorrow. It wasn't really, it was something else, but that's what it meant, and more surprising than two humans agreeing to name a small baby Sorrow was that he didn't know what his name meant. He could have guessed. I could have guessed. You would have guessed too if you knew him, drinking of his tears from flowers that looked like sad lips and swollen genitals, cupping rain and insects, darlings, carnivorous darlings. He was young enough that I could see him as perfect archetype, his skateboard was symbol. He asked for me to read to him, like he thought he could hear sex and mama in my voice.

Which is true, I didn't know which voice to talk to him in, I could have nursed him from a thousand breasts I have grown for these very moments. This is also true, undress me, you will see. Rows and rows of breasts, a monster of give and gaze. If you have ever nursed someone you know, you understand it is not sexual but it blurs lines so deeply that the next time you let someone touch you, you confuse mothering for fucking.

Especially the sad boys, the ones who might just float away, a fish or a map maker, bound by routes you do not know. So, when you come at me like a fog bank, I think of a girl and that slip of land that ran below the cypress ridge, the way she and I would find warm pockets of nightness, and twirl in them, so aware of a moment unfolding as flower. Aware in a way that only 15 year-old girls can be aware to the life of flowers.

The fog pressed us in, formed a room that glowed from the inside out. There was an owl, a badger, two deer. Everything in fog is peripheral. Fog is love, if that's not obvious. The way you can walk next to a badger with your ankles showing. And love is attention, we know this because we study the body movement of Tarkovsky listening to poetry.

But me and this girl, we would feel the pockets of warm as we maneuvered through the darkness in creature form. I think we were animals, for everyone wanted to pet us. We knew that we were swimming in fragile river sky, a current of trail and road, a dead skunk, leering men in cars made of 'Come here, let me take you home.' We step backwards, disappearing together, wearing slips.

I wish I could have held her hand and said: In forty years we will move past all the Sorrows. We will have children marked by people who left us but mostly marked by us. We will bury our pets over and over again looking for that feeling that you get only from dogs and fog banks and girls who say marry me, marry me, marry me, our love is pure.

The Everlasting Eulogy of Lush

Lush being one of my words intimate, because
I have lived with ferns,
their dim undersides holding
rows of circled spores
laid neatly in shadow, dust sex and wind blow.

I am lush sideways salivation,
the way I creep through your orchard raising skirt,
Luh, the sound of moan with loop,
Ush, the last whisper, death rattle of lonely, pretty in creek walk,
I give you lip.

You come at me Mountain,
our home a wood field where deer go to die,
we fill our stove with bones, cloven hooves, broth,
steam marrow against winter, the glass cries drip.
'It's the wind,' you say, 'trying to find me to you.'

I am lush slut spoke softly
your bottom lip dragging,
there was never any poetry without you in it,
there was never any poetry,
there was never.

Everyone has a song,
But we have a wet, drunken word,
born of walk and bed.

25 Things I Want During a Pandemic: A List, Also a Love Poem

1. I want to take a bath with you and watch the water turn dirty
    so that we can remark on the elusiveness of film, remembering
    the prettiest reflections we have found
2. I want to drive you across that highway that splits the marsh
    into northwest and southeast and find bodies of birds so white
    we forget their counterparts in cloud
3. I want to declare you quietly to the trees, who are me, and watch
    the enveloping of fog, who is you
4. I want to drag whales into the bedroom to ensure humility in the
    face of hearts larger than ours
5. I want to dress as a crying vampire with tears so pretty on my face
    that you forget joke
6. I want to write origin story with you, masked
7. I want to eat every meal you cook because I have always been
    starving
8. I want to collect your mistakes and build instruments of them to
    play back to you luthier and residency
9. I want to listen to your ocean as we sleep as if I am submarine, your
    tubes an anchor
10. I want to sit up over you as your body grips trachea, nudging you
    back into breath
11. I want the dairy, the tract home, the door of breastbone
12. I want to walk to the land of old with you
13. I want to walk wet face with you
14. I want to walk creek with you
15. I want to go back into time so that I can cut and thank every
    human who has caused you harm, for I want to protect you but
    love you as you are
16. I want to look at you in snow melt
17. I want to look at you in desert wake
18. I want to look at you in swamp, on boat, as old as you can be
19. I want nothing more than this
20. I want you to dress my body in post-it notes and hang dead leaves
    from my hair so that you know the world has reckoned us
    symbology and storm as form of trinket, altar
21. I want to count the last dying animals with you, to see the deer lay
    her head down in heat as we cry, grieving, the sky one side of a
    blood orange

22. I want you to never unwrap your arms from around me
23. I want you to never forget that you have always been two blocks away
24. I want you as painter
25. I want the animal of us in den, digging hole, as we dream back the fox, the bobcat, the love of vulture pretty

About the Author

Kelly Gray (she/her/hers) is a writer and educator living among the quietest and tallest trees in the world on occupied Coast Miwok land, nine miles and seven fence posts away from the ocean, deep within fire country. She has one perfect cat, two spoiled yet emotionally bereft dogs, and a beautiful human child who is the recipient of her lifelong love letter, a work still in progress. Gray is fortunate enough to create a home with her love, painter Gage Opdenbrouw, among fog banks and the shadow of flowers. Gray's writing has been selected for publication by literary journals such as *Atticus Review, Lunch Ticket, Passages North, Wildroof Journal, The Normal School, Bracken Magazine, Pithead Chapel* and more. Her forthcoming play, *Beautiful Monsters*, will be produced by Left Edge Theater in the summer of 2021. You can watch, listen or read more of Gray's work at writekgray.com.

Acknowledgements

The author wishes to thank the following publications where these poems have previously appeared or are forthcoming, sometimes in varying form:

"Augury" and "The Hush of the Switch Blade" ~ *CULTURAL WEEKLY*
"Blue Blood of a Bolete" ~ *Quiet Lightening*, 2020
"Celebration of Vultures" ~ *Bracken Magazine*, 2020
"Her Name is Amy" ~ *3Elements Review*
"Home of Seamstress" ~ *Ghost City Press*, 2021
"Keeping Apparitions" ~ *Burning House Press*, 2020
"The Fox as Form" ~ *write, bitch, write!*, 2020
"On Becoming a Whale" ~ *Bracken Magazine*, 2020
"Pulling Bastard" ~ *The Nervous Breakdown*, 2020
"The Everlasting Eulogy of Lush" ~ *Passenger's Journal*, 2021
"The Fish as Healer" ~ *The Normal School*, 2020
"The Hart" ~ *River Teeth*, 2021
"The Last Story" ~ forthcoming from *Midway Journal*
"When the Shooter Comes; Instructions for My Daughter" ~ *Quiet Lightening*, 2020

Acknowledgements, Flowers

I would like to write flowers into ink for all the people who have supported me writing this book. You read my manuscript, offered me critique, encouraged me, connected me to resources, and opportunity, and I bring you blooms, roots and seeds. Thank you to the ghosts, spirits, wild creatures and past entanglements for allowing me to retell stories that do not only belong to me. For those who are nameless in my process, I offer you a branch of ceanothus on the foggiest of mornings. Thank you to all my friends who received poems over text message in the deep of night, read them and then responded, I want to bring you wild wood roses when you wake. For Sandra Lloyd, an obscene bouquet of Cala Lilies to place on your altar of love. For Rhona Berens, a rambling armful of sweet peas. For Shannon Hanks Mackey, I'll dig up Mandrake and dress it in bonnet for you. For Dani Burlison, Belladonna and Hemlock, you'll know what to do. For Doug Baulos, my twin of shoe and ink, dried daffodils and moth wings. For Linda Flaherty Haltmaier, the Swamp-rose mallows are for you. For Michelle Tea, a bush of bougainvillea of the brightest magenta. Freddie Blooms, look at the coastal buckwheat, you'll see it smiling. Catherine Pierce, my sweet, Datura in the apple orchard on a full moon, pluck, pluck. For my father, Dennis Gray and Karletta Moniz, watch the tulips become outrageously stunning as they age. For Rich Ferguson, that daisy that is pushing up through the cement, that's for you. Eric Morago and Moon Tide Press, I'll plant a garden of papyrus in the brightest of bogs in your honor. For Makenzie Burt, girl, let's just eat donuts. Anna Reiner, ever since we were kids you told me I should write a book, and now that we are here, I want to hang garlands of violet lilacs from your windows. For my love, Gage, who reminds me daily of the life of an artist and shadow land, black peonies and wild cucumber vines. And lastly, because it is the most important, for London Abigail, may you always walk among the windflowers, one of each color, for your belief in me. You are my most favorite bloom of all.

Also Available from Moon Tide Press

Patrons

Moon Tide Press would like to thank the following people for their support in helping publish the finest poetry from the Southern California region. To sign up as a patron, visit www.moontidepress.com or send an email to publisher@moontidepress.com.

Anonymous
Robin Axworthy
Conner Brenner
Nicole Connolly
Bill Cushing
Susan Davis
Peggy Dobreer
Dennis Gowans
Alexis Rhone Fancher
Hanalena Fennel
Half Off Books & Brad T. Cox
Donna Hilbert
Jim & Vicky Hoggatt
Michael Kramer
Ron Koertge & Bianca Richards
Gary Jacobelly
Ray & Christi Lacoste
Zachary & Tammy Locklin
Lincoln McElwee
David McIntire
José Enrique Medina
Michael Miller & Rachanee Srisavasdi
Michelle & Robert Miller
Ronny & Richard Morago
Terri Niccum
Andrew November
Jeremy Ra
Luke & Mia Salazar
Jennifer Smith
Andrew Turner
Rex Wilder
Mariano Zaro
Wes Bryan Zwick

Made in the USA
Monee, IL
08 September 2021

76726775R10042